UNLEASH YOUR FINANCIAL FREEDOM

Your Guide to Smart Money Management

Table of contents

Chapter 1. INTRODUCTION:

In the present speedy purchaser-driven world, the compulsion to spend pointlessly can be ever-present, prompting monetary pressure and unsteadiness. This guide investigates reasonable methodologies to break liberated from the hold of pointless ways of managing money. From making a spending plan to developing careful buying choices, we'll dive into the instruments and methods that engage you to assume command over your funds. By following these means, you'll protect your monetary prosperity as well as make ready for a safer and prosperous future. How about we set out on this excursion to monetary obligation and financial opportunity.

Chapter 2: CREATING A BUDGET

In the journey to vanquish superfluous ways of managing money, making a spending plan fills in as a primary point of support. This part dives into the fundamental advances expected for viable planning.

2.1 Following Pay and Costs: The most important phase in this planning odyssey is grasping your monetary scene. Track each dollar acquired and spent. This fastidious examination uncovers spending examples and regions where your well deserved cash may be releasing away inconspicuous. Furnished with this information, you're better prepared to settle on informed choices.

2.2 Distributing Assets: When you have an unmistakable image of your monetary inflow and surge, now is the ideal time to prudently dispense reserves. Focus on necessities like bills and reserve funds prior to distributing optional pay for needs. This proactive methodology guarantees that your cash works for you, assisting you with accomplishing your monetary objectives.

By dominating these planning essentials, you'll be on the way to monetary dependability and freedom from the shackles of incautious spending.

Chapter 3: PRIORITIZING NEEDS OVER WANTS

In the excursion towards monetary judiciousness, knowing among needs and needs is a significant expertise. This section enlightens the meaning of focusing on basics over wants.

In a world overflowing with tempting items and encounters, it's not difficult to obscure the line between what we really want and what we simply desire. Be that as it may, by embracing a requirements first mindset, you'll encourage monetary discipline.

This section dives into methodologies for recognizing needs, like lodging, utilities, and food, and needs, which include unnecessary buys and guilty pleasures. By figuring out how to fulfill your necessities prior to enjoying needs, you'll brace your monetary establishment and diminish the charm of pointless spending.

Find how this change in outlook can prompt long haul monetary strength and flexibility against hasty buys, at last pushing you towards your monetary objectives.

Chapter 4: SETTING SAVING GOALS

Chasing after monetary soundness, Part 4 spotlights on the crucial stage of defining investment funds objectives. By portraying your monetary yearnings, you outline a course towards financial obligation.

Investment funds objectives act as directing reference points on your monetary excursion. This section will dive into the meaning of characterizing clear targets, whether they include making a secret stash, putting something aside for a fantasy excursion, or anticipating retirement.

Figure out how to lay out Savvy (Explicit, Quantifiable, Reachable, Significant, and Time-bound) objectives, empowering you to dispense assets successfully and remain propelled. Find the force of steady commitments towards your investment funds targets, cultivating monetary security and decreasing the charm of negligible spending.

As you leave on the way of laying out investment funds objectives, you'll furnish yourself with the devices important to shorten pointless costs and guarantee a prosperous monetary future.

Chapter 5: TRACKING EXPENSES

In the journey for monetary care, Section 5 investigates the significance of following costs. By fastidiously checking your spending, you gain priceless bits of knowledge into your monetary propensities.

This section dives into functional procedures for recording each consumption, from everyday espresso rushes to significant buys. Through constant following, you'll uncover spending designs, recognize areas of possible reserve funds, and gain a thorough perspective on your monetary wellbeing.

Find how different apparatuses, for example, planning applications or straightforward bookkeeping sheets, can work on the cycle. By remaining careful in checking your costs, you'll be better prepared to control pointless spending and divert assets towards your monetary objectives.

As you embrace the act of cost following, you'll take a huge step towards monetary control and the acknowledgment of your monetary desires.

Chapter 6: AVOIDING IMPULSE BUYING

In the fight against superfluous spending, Part 6 tends to the test of motivation purchasing. We investigate methodologies to oppose the appeal of unconstrained buys and settle on informed monetary decisions.

Drive purchasing can prompt monetary laments and obstruct your advancement towards monetary objectives. This part offers experiences into perceiving triggers for imprudent spending and gives procedures to check these inclinations.

Figure out how to carry out a "stop and reflect" approach prior to making buys, and find the benefit of making shopping records and adhering to them. By becoming amazing at careful spending, you can recapture command over your funds and channel your assets towards the main thing.

As you dive into the systems introduced in this part, you'll acquire the devices important to battle rash spending and fabricate a safer monetary future.

Chapter 7: LIMITING CREDIT CARD USE

This section tends to the basic part of controlling charge card use to keep up with monetary solidness. Visas can be advantageous yet can likewise prompt obligation in the event that not oversaw shrewdly.

Gain proficiency with the significance of mindful Visa use, remembering taking care of balances for full every month to keep away from exorbitant interest charges. Find methodologies to restrict Visa use, like leaving cards at home for pointless buys.

Investigate the advantages of setting spending limits on your charge cards and understanding the terms and expenses related with them. By dominating these procedures, you'll keep away from pointless obligation and interest installments, permitting your monetary assets to help you out.

Toward the finish of this part, you'll be furnished with the information and procedures expected to utilize charge cards mindfully and diminish the gamble of pointless spending and monetary strain.

Chapter 8: COOKING AT HOME

In the midst of the quest for monetary reasonability, Part 8 stresses the benefits of cooking at home. Find how setting up your feasts can prompt massive expense reserve funds while advancing better wellbeing and monetary prosperity.

This part investigates the advantages of home-prepared feasts, including decreased eating costs and better command over fixings. Learn commonsense tips for dinner arranging, shopping for food, and improving your kitchen space to make cooking at home more helpful.

Uncover the delight of exploring different avenues regarding recipes and embracing a better way of life. As you dig into this part, you'll understand that cooking at home sustains your monetary dependability as well as permits you to enjoy the kinds of independence from the rat race.

Chapter 9: REDUCING SUBSCRIPTION

In the journey for monetary effectiveness, Part 9 spotlights on the significance of lessening memberships. The cutting edge world offers a plenty of membership administrations, from streaming stages to month to month enrollments, which can discreetly disintegrate your spending plan.

This section looks at the meaning of assessing and pruning pointless memberships. Figure out how to recognize memberships that never again offer some benefit or line up with your needs.

Find commonsense techniques for dropping, minimizing, or imparting memberships to loved ones to lessen costs while as yet partaking in the advantages of these administrations. By diminishing memberships, you'll let loose assets for additional fundamental parts of your life and monetary objectives.

As you dive into the substance of this section, you'll acquire the instruments and experiences to clean up your monetary responsibilities and recapture command over your ways of managing money.

Chapter 10: BUILDING AN EMERGENCY FUND

This section digs into the basic part of building a secret stash, a fundamental monetary wellbeing net. A just-in-case account gives genuine serenity and monetary security in surprising circumstances.

Realize the reason why having a rainy day account is pivotal and how to lay out one. Investigate pragmatic methods for defining investment funds objectives, computerizing commitments, and picking the right record for your asset.

Find the suggested size of your rainy day account, which can cover startling costs like doctor's visit expenses, vehicle fixes, or employment misfortune. By making and reliably adding to your rainy day account, you'll safeguard yourself from monetary difficulty and diminish the requirement for impromptu, pointless spending.

As you progress through this section, you'll acquire an unmistakable comprehension of the significance of a backup stash and the means expected to construct one, guaranteeing you're more ready for life's monetary curves.

Chapter 11: AVOIDING RETAIL THERAPY

In the excursion towards monetary care, Part 11 tends to the normal entanglement of retail treatment. This survival strategy, while immediately calming, can prompt rash and pointless spending.

This part investigates the brain research behind retail treatment and its effect on your funds. Figure out how to perceive triggers that lead to such way of behaving, whether it's pressure, fatigue, or profound pain.

Find better choices to retail treatment, for example, care activities, side interests, or looking for help from loved ones. By developing close to home versatility and resolving basic issues, you can decrease the dependence on retail treatment and its unfriendly monetary results.

As you dig into this section, you'll obtain important experiences into breaking the pattern of profound spending, liberating yourself from the bait of imprudent buys, and sustaining your general prosperity.

Chapter 12: AUTOMATING SAVINGS

Chasing monetary soundness, Section 12 digs into the influential idea of robotizing reserve funds. Computerizing your reserve funds can be a distinct advantage, guaranteeing steady advancement towards your monetary objectives.

This section investigates the benefits of setting up programmed moves to your bank account. Figure out how to lay out a consistent cycle that coordinates a piece of your pay into investment funds before you even get an opportunity to spend it.

Find the different strategies and instruments accessible to mechanize investment funds, including boss supported retirement plans, direct store parts, and planning applications. By focusing on investment funds and computerizing the cycle, you'll consistently create financial momentum without the requirement for steady discipline.

As you submerge yourself in this section, you'll get the information and devices important to develop your reserve funds, bracing your monetary future and diminishing the enticement of superfluous spending easily.

Chapter 13: STAYING INFORMED

In the powerful universe of individual accounting, Section 13 underscores the basic job of remaining informed. To pursue informed monetary choices and stay away from pointless spending, it is crucial for progressing instruction.

This section investigates different ways of remaining informed about monetary issues, including keeping awake to-date on financial patterns, speculation amazing open doors, and changes in charge regulations. Find the worth of respectable monetary news sources, books, webcasts, and courses.

Gain proficiency with the significance of grasping essential monetary ideas, for example, financing costs, expansion, and speculation techniques. By expanding your monetary proficiency, you'll be better prepared to use wise judgment that line up with your drawn out objectives.

As you draw in with the substance of this section, you'll acquire the devices and assets expected to explore the always changing monetary scene unhesitatingly, guaranteeing your monetary prosperity and diminishing the gamble of superfluous spending.

Chapter 14: REVIEW AND ADJUSTMENTS

In the continuous excursion of monetary reasonability, Part 14 highlights the meaning of normal survey and change. Your monetary arrangement ought to develop with your life conditions and objectives.

This part investigates the act of occasionally looking into your spending plan, reserve funds objectives, and speculation systems. Figure out how to evaluate your advancement, distinguish regions for development, and adjust your monetary arrangement appropriately.

Find the significance of adaptability in your monetary methodology. Life is loaded with startling exciting bends in the road, and your monetary procedure ought to have the option to smoothly oblige changes.

By drawing in with the substance of this part, you'll foster the abilities to proactively deal with your monetary excursion, guaranteeing that you remain focused with your goals and keep up with discipline in staying away from superfluous spending.

CONCLUSION

As we arrive at the finish of this extensive aide on staying away from pointless ways of managing money and cultivating monetary reasonability, obviously independence from the rat race is accessible for anybody able to assume command over their funds.

All through the sections, you've investigated fundamental ideas, for example, planning, focusing on needs over needs, laying out investment funds objectives, and some more. These standards, when applied reliably, enable you to pursue informed choices, check incautious spending, and secure your monetary future.

Recollect that monetary obligation is a deep rooted venture. By carrying out the methodologies examined in this aide and keeping a promise to monetary care, you can accomplish your monetary objectives, fabricate a hearty wellbeing net, and diminish the charm of negligible spending.

At last, the way to monetary soundness is cleared with discipline, information, and diligence. With these devices available to you, you're exceptional to explore the difficulties of dealing with your funds shrewdly and embracing the compensations of a protected and prosperous monetary future.

www.ingramcontent.com/pod-product-compliance
Lightning Source LLC
Chambersburg PA
CBHW072228290526
45794CB00007B/2931